SHOW-ME-HOW

I Can Play Games

Fun-to-play games
for younger children

PETRA BOASE

LORENZ BOOKS

This edition published by Lorenz Books

Lorenz Books is an imprint
of Anness Publishing Limited
Hermes House
88–89 Blackfriars Road
London SE1 8HA

This edition distributed in Canada
by Raincoast Books
8680 Cambie Street
Vancouver
British Columbia V6P 6M9

ISBN 0 7548 0225 6

A CIP catalogue record for this book
is available from the British Library.

Publisher: Joanna Lorenz
Senior Editor, Children's Books: Sue Grabham
Editor: Charlotte Evans
Photographer: John Freeman
Designer: Rachael Stone

PLEASE NOTE
The amount of help needed from adults
will depend on the abilities and ages of
the children following the projects.
However, we advise that adult supervision
is vital when the project calls for the use of
sharp scissors or other utensils. Always
keep potentially harmful tools well out of
the reach of young children.

ACKNOWLEDGEMENTS
The Publishers would like to thank the
following children, their parents and
Walnut Tree Walk Primary School:
Nathanael Arnott-Davies, Hazel Askew,
Anthony Bainbridge, Shaunagh Brown,
James Danso, Rachel Deacon Smith,
Joanne Fleck, Mary Fleck, Fawwaz
Abdul Ghany, Zach King, Georgina
Nipah, Rebecca Quayson, Charlie
Emilyn Ray, Jinsamu Shimizu, Tom
Swaine Jameson, Simon Paul Anthony
Thexton and Sophie Louise Viner.

Printed in Hong Kong/China

© Anness Publishing Limited 1997, 1999
10 9 8 7 6 5 4 3 2 1

 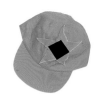

Contents

Introduction

Games are such fun to play whether you are at home or at school, with a group of friends or on your own. They are a great way of making new friends and getting lots of healthy exercise.

You probably know lots of games already and you may even recognize some of the games in this book. Other games will be new to you, so you might need a little practice before you become expert at them. For some of the games you will need to make some simple pieces of equipment, but they are very easy to make and great fun to do. All the games have step-by-step pictures to show you exactly what to do. There are also suggestions on how to score. In time, you might want to make up your own rules for certain games or even invent some games of your own.

Games are a good way to get exercise.

Where to play
Many of these games can be played both indoors and outdoors. If you are playing indoors, make sure any breakable objects are put away and that you have a large space to play in. Soft, lightweight balls should be used indoors. When playing outdoors, always tell an adult where you will be.

What to wear
Shorts, leggings and a T-shirt are good clothes for playing games in as they let you move freely. It is not a good idea to play games in your best clothes – you do not want them ruined!

When you are playing the games, especially those which involve lots of running and jumping, wear shoes with rubber soles and toe protection. Check that shoelaces are tied and that the laces are not dragging on the ground. Summer sandals are not sensible shoes to play games in, but trainers and gym shoes are ideal.

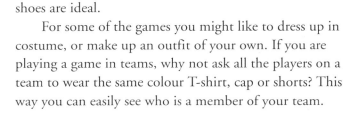
Play in loose, comfy clothes.

For some of the games you might like to dress up in costume, or make up an outfit of your own. If you are playing a game in teams, why not ask all the players on a team to wear the same colour T-shirt, cap or shorts? This way you can easily see who is a member of your team.

Making equipment
The equipment you will need to play some of the games is not expensive or difficult to make.

Most of the projects use materials that you will find at home, such as old plastic bottles, card from cereal packets, newspapers and garden canes. You will be amazed by what you can make with such simple everyday objects! You will also be helping to save the Earth's resources by recycling materials that would otherwise be thrown away.

Before you set to work on making any project, ask an adult for permission to use special items. If the project you are making is very messy, it is important to cover the surface you are working on

Before you start playing a game, make sure you have all the equipment you need.

Papier mâché can be messy to make, so wear an old T-shirt and protect your work surface.

Leave papier mâché to dry thoroughly before painting it.

with newspaper, scrap paper or some old material. It is also a good idea to wear an old T-shirt or painting overall to protect your clothes.

When you are ready to start, make sure you have read the equipment list for each project and laid out everything you need on your work surface. Read through the instructions carefully so that you know what to do. Always ask an adult to do anything that needs sharp scissors or a compass. If you are unsure about what to do, ask an adult or a friend to help you.

Some of the projects will involve gluing. It is very important to allow the glue to dry thoroughly, sometimes overnight, before using your home-made equipment. This also applies to pieces of equipment that have been painted. When you have finished making a project or playing a game, always clear away everything you have used and remember to tidy up after yourself.

If you concentrate and try hard, you are sure to be a winner!

It is sporting to congratulate the winner at the end of a game.

How to play

All the games in this book are easy to understand and simple to set up. You do not always need a large group of friends to play with as many of the games can be played by just two people or on your own.

Before you start, however, there are a few things you should do.

Nobody likes a bad loser!

1. Carefully read through the list of materials and tools you will need to play the game.
2. Read through the step-by-step instructions slowly and look at the photographs so that you have a clear idea of what you will be doing.
3. Assemble everything you need before starting on an activity.

The most important thing to remember when playing games is that they are meant to be fun. They are not competitions to find who is the best or the fastest. So, get active, have fun and keep smiling!

Bat template

To play the games on page 14 you will need to make a bat for each player. Use the template opposite and follow these instructions to transfer the template on to a piece of card.

1 Place a sheet of tracing paper over the template pattern and hold it in position with your spare hand. Carefully draw around the shape with a soft pencil.

2 Take the tracing paper off the template and turn it over. The lines you have just drawn should be face down on the table. Scribble over the outline with your pencil.

3 Turn the tracing paper over again and place it on a piece of card, scribble-side down. Draw over the outline of the pattern firmly. This will transfer the picture on to the card.

4 Remove the tracing paper and make sure all the pattern has been transferred. Carefully cut out the shape with scissors. You now have your own template to draw around.

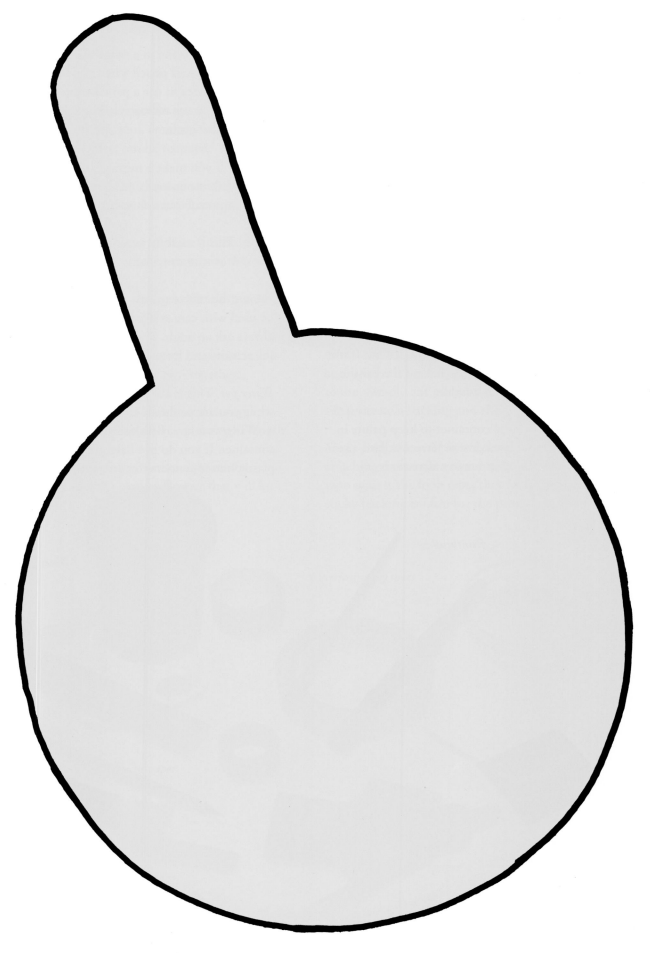

Sticky back Velcro

Card

Noughts and Crosses

This is a giant version of the game normally played on paper with a pen or pencil. It is a game for two players and can be played both indoors and outdoors. If you are playing the game in the playground you could draw the squares with chalk. If you do not have any coloured paper to make the noughts and crosses with, use pieces of newspaper or cardboard boxes instead.

Sophie has won this game of Noughts and Crosses by putting her three noughts in a row.

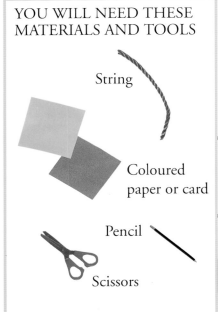

YOU WILL NEED THESE
MATERIALS AND TOOLS

String

Coloured
paper or card

Pencil

Scissors

1 Carefully draw out the noughts and the crosses on large pieces of coloured paper. You will need to draw five of each shape.

2 Cut out the noughts and crosses with a pair of scissors. There is a lot to be done, so ask a friend or adult to help you.

3 Lay out the board for the game with four even lengths of string, or draw it in chalk if you are playing it in the playground.

4 One player is noughts and the other is crosses. Toss a coin to decide who starts. The winner places their first shape in one of the boxes.

5 The second player then places their first shape in another box.

6 The game continues with each player taking it in turns to place a shape. Each player is trying to get three shapes in a line while stopping the other from doing so.

7 The first player to make a line with their shape is the winner and starts the next game. The overall winner is whoever wins the most games.

Make your noughts and crosses in different colours. The larger they are, the larger your board will have to be to fit them all on!

Ready, Steady, Go!

Races are great fun at parties – these races might make you laugh so much that you forget you are in a race! Races are best played outdoors. Before you start, make sure you have all the equipment ready and that you have asked an adult's permission to borrow it. It is a good idea to have someone as a referee. The referee tells everyone when to start and calls out the winner.

Shaunagh and her best friend are in the Three Legged Race. Before starting, they needed to work out which leg they would both begin on.

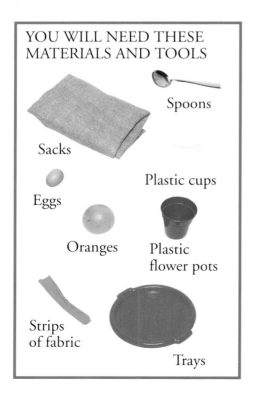

YOU WILL NEED THESE MATERIALS AND TOOLS

Sacks

Spoons

Eggs

Plastic cups

Oranges

Plastic flower pots

Strips of fabric

Trays

1 **Egg and Spoon Race** - Balance an egg on a spoon and run to the finish line. Whoever crosses the line first with their egg is the winner.

2 **Flower Pot Race** - Balance a flower pot on the head and run or walk to the finish line. If the flower pot falls off, go back to the beginning.

3 **Sack Race** - Climb inside a sack and then run or jump in the sack to the finish line. The winner is the first person to cross the finish line.

4 **Water Race** - Place eight plastic cups filled with water on a tray. Run to the finish line with the tray, trying not to spill too much water.

5 **Three Legged Race** - Race in pairs with your ankles tied together. The referee could tie you together with a strip of fabric.

6 Put your arms around each other's shoulders and try to run together as fast as you can. The first pair to cross the finish line are the winners.

7 **Oranges and Knees Race** - Place an orange between your knees and run to the finish line. If you drop the orange, go back to the beginning.

To help you get to the finish line without tripping, pull the sack up tight and push your toes into the corners of the sack.

Ball Games

These are great fun to play on your own or with a friend. All ball games need lots of practice, but remember to concentrate and keep your eye on the ball. To make the bat, trace the template on page 7.

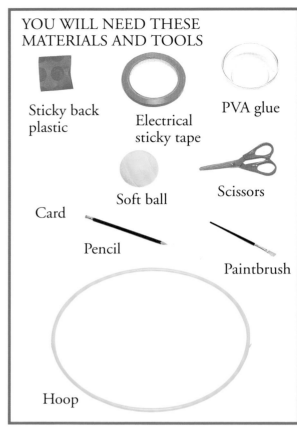

YOU WILL NEED THESE
MATERIALS AND TOOLS

Sticky back plastic

Electrical sticky tape

PVA glue

Soft ball

Scissors

Card

Pencil

Paintbrush

Hoop

Fawwaz made these great bats so that he and a friend could get in some tennis practice. See how hard they are looking at the ball and not at their bats? This will help them to hit the ball better.

1 Draw around the bat template on a piece of card. For each bat you will need two pieces of card. Glue the two pieces together and leave to dry.

2 Cut a piece of sticky back plastic slightly bigger than the bat. Stick it to one side of the bat and snip the edges. Fold down the edges.

3 Cut another piece of sticky back plastic exactly the same size as the bat and stick it to the other side. Use electrical tape to decorate the bat.

4 Use the bats to hit a soft ball back and forth between you. If you miss the ball you get a penalty point. The first player to get ten points loses.

5 Ball Games can be played on your own. First throw a soft ball high enough into the air to be able to clap your hands and catch the ball again.

6 Then throw the ball high enough into the air to be able to clap your hands and click your fingers before catching the ball again.

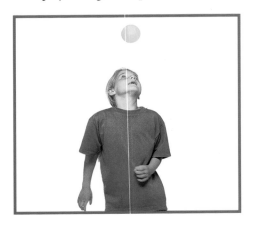

7 This is hard, but give it a go! Throw the ball into the air and clap your hands, click your fingers and twist your body before catching it.

8 Practise twisting in a hoop. When you are ready, throw the ball into the air and clap your hands and twist in the hoop before catching the ball.

Only use a soft, very lightweight ball with your home-made bats.

Tied up in Knots

This game can be played outdoors on grass or indoors on carpet. The aim is not to fall over and get tied up in knots. Play the game in bare feet or socks and make up your own rules to make it as hard or as easy as you like. Beware – this game will make you laugh!

YOU WILL NEED THESE
MATERIALS AND TOOLS

150cm x 150cm piece of
strong white cloth or calico

Felt

Paintbrush

Coloured fabric
for the fruits

Coloured paper

Compass and pencil

PVA glue

White and
coloured card

Scissors

Paper fastener

Rebecca is the acrobatic champ of this game! If you do not have fabric for the fruits, use fabric paint to paint the fruit on to the cloth. Remember to ask for permission before you do this.

1 Draw a circle on some white card with a compass. Cut out and glue on to a square of card. Ask an adult to make a hole in the centre.

2 Cut out an apple, a strawberry, an orange and a lemon from coloured paper and glue them on to the circle. Cut out an arrow from coloured card.

3 Push a paper fastener through the end of the arrow and the middle of the circle. Turn over the card and fold the back of the paper fastener out flat.

4 Make two strawberries, one apple, two lemons and one orange from coloured fabric and felt. Glue these on to the white cloth in rows of three.

5 When the glue is dry, spin the arrow on the fruity board and see where it stops. The first player then places a foot or a hand on that fruit.

6 Spin the arrow again and where it stops, the second player puts a foot or a hand on that fruit.

7 The game continues and the players take it in turns to move. However, once a hand or a foot is on a fruit it must not be moved.

8 Try not to tie yourself into knots. You will fall over and be out of the game. The winner is the player who does not lose their balance and fall over.

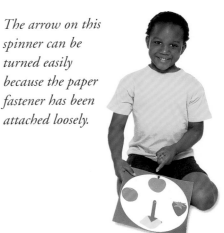

The arrow on this spinner can be turned easily because the paper fastener has been attached loosely.

Skipping Games

Only play these games and exercises outdoors as you will need lots of space. If you do not already have your own skipping rope this project shows you how to make your own. The fun part of playing skipping games is making up your own rhymes to sing along to with your friends. If you have never skipped before, do not panic – just keep practising and you will soon be an expert!

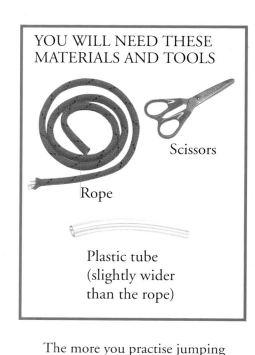

YOU WILL NEED THESE MATERIALS AND TOOLS

Scissors

Rope

Plastic tube (slightly wider than the rope)

The more you practise jumping over the rope, the faster you will get. Try not to take off!

1 Cut a piece of rope 2m long. Cut two lengths of plastic tubing, each about 12cm long. Thread each end of the rope through a piece of tubing.

2 Tie the rope in a knot either side of the plastic tubing to make the handles. You can decorate them with electrical sticky tape if you like.

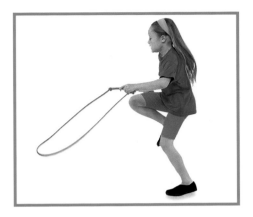

3 Start off your warm up by stepping quickly or skipping over the rope. If you hold the rope too high, you will make this exercise very hard to do!

4 Now hop on one foot over the rope. Have a small competition with your friends to see who can hop for the longest without stopping.

5 If you feel energetic, try jumping over the rope with lots of small jumps one after the other. How many can you do without stopping?

6 Ask two friends to swing the rope backwards and forwards. When they have got into a rhythm, run into the rope and start skipping. After some practice, try hopping.

7 The ultimate challenge is to do a skipping routine with two or more friends. Make sure you all skip, jump and hop at the same time.

For the skipping games where there are three or more players, you will have to make a longer skipping rope.

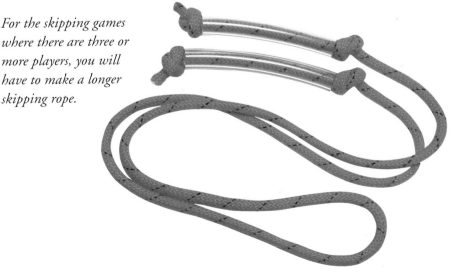

Paper Plate Volleyball

This is a fun energetic game and can be played both indoors and outdoors with two or more players. If you are outdoors, put up a net using a piece of string. To score, each player could start with 21 points. Every time you miss the ball you lose a point. Keep playing until one player loses all their points.

Nathanael looks very happy to have won a game of Paper Plate Volleyball!

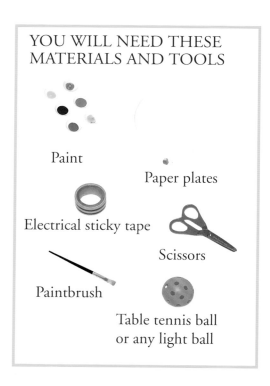

YOU WILL NEED THESE
MATERIALS AND TOOLS

Paint

Paper plates

Electrical sticky tape

Scissors

Paintbrush

Table tennis ball
or any light ball

1 For each bat you will need two paper plates. Paint the underside of each plate a plain colour and leave the paint to dry completely.

2 Paint colourful patterns or funny cartoon faces on the painted side of each plate. Leave the paint to dry completely again.

3 Fasten the two plates together with pieces of colourful electrical sticky tape, leaving a gap just big enough for your hand to slide inside.

4 Slide your hand inside the paper plate bat and you are ready to play. Toss a coin to see which player will serve first.

5 The server hits the ball to their partner using a paper plate bat. With practice you will be able to judge how hard you must hit the ball.

6 The other player hits the ball back to the server before it touches the ground. Carry on hitting the ball between you for as long as you can.

7 When a player misses the ball and it lands on the ground, that player loses a point. The game continues until one player has lost all their points.

These paper plate bats have been painted in bright, colourful patterns.

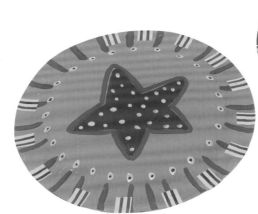

Ratcatcher

This game is best played outdoors with lots of friends. Choose someone to be the ratcatcher and the rest of you are the rats. The ratcatcher is very greedy and wants to catch all the rats. To escape from the clutches of the ratcatcher, the rats must be nimble. Whenever the ratcatcher gets close to a rat, the ratcatcher steals its tail. The one lucky rat who still has a tail at the end of the game becomes the new ratcatcher.

YOU WILL NEED THESE
MATERIALS AND TOOLS

Tissue paper

Shaunagh was the last rat left at the end of this game, so she is the winner. You have to be quick to avoid the hungry ratcatcher!

1 To make the tails for the rats, roll pieces of tissue paper or newspaper into long tubes. Twist them to look like long wiry tails.

2 Each rat tucks the end of a tail into the waist of their shorts. The rats then scurry in all directions to stay out of reach of you know who!

3 The greedy ratcatcher starts to chase the rats. The ratcatcher will have to be quick, nimble and sneaky to catch the fleeing rats.

4 The rats are scared of being caught and try to run away from the ratcatcher. Try twisting and turning to stop the ratcatcher grabbing your tail.

5 The ratcatcher catches a rat by pulling out its tail. The unlucky rat is now out of the game. Before the ratcatcher can chase the other rats, the stolen tail must be tucked into the waist of the ratcatcher's shorts.

6 The more tails the ratcatcher has, the greedier the ratcatcher gets. The game continues until there is only one rat left with a tail.

7 The winner is the last lucky rat not to lose its tail to the ratcatcher. The last rat then becomes the new ratcatcher and the game begins again.

You will need a tissue paper tail for each rat. If you do not have any tissue paper, use newspaper instead.

23

Hot Potato and Cheese Sandwich

These two games are fun to play at a party, where you could dress up in fancy dress. They could also be played at school in the playground at breaktime.

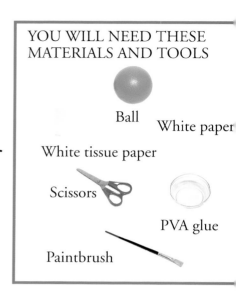

Ball   White paper

White tissue paper

Scissors

PVA glue

Paintbrush

These three friends are playing Cheese Sandwich. To catch the crisp green apple, the boy in the centre has to jump very high indeed!

1 **Hot Potato** - To make the chef's hat, cut a piece of paper 30cm x 60cm. Make it into a tube to fit around your head and glue the ends.

2 Glue a piece of tissue paper to the inside edge of one end of the tube (you might need to ask an adult to help you). Leave the chef's hat to dry.

3 Stand in a ring around the chef. The chef aims the hot potato (the ball) at the players' feet. The players jump up on the spot to avoid the ball.

4 If the ball hits a player's feet, they are out. The winner is the player whose feet are not burnt by the hot potato. They become the new chef.

5 **Cheese Sandwich** - Choose two players to be the bread and one to be the cheese in the middle. The ball is a green apple that the cheese wants.

6 The sandwich players throw the ball to each other trying not to let the cheese catch it.

7 If the cheese is lucky enough to catch the green apple, the sandwich player who was last to throw the ball becomes the new cheese.

Use a beach ball or a football to play these games. If you do not have the materials to make the chef's hat, you can wear an ordinary hat instead.

Hopscotch

This game is best played in the playground. Use chalk to mark out the pitch. You can keep score in this game by awarding points. If you successfully hop and jump up and down the pitch without falling over, you score the same points as the square your pebble landed on. You cannot stand in the square your pebble landed on to pick it up. Make the squares quite large so that you do not step on the lines.

YOU WILL NEED THESE
MATERIALS AND TOOLS

Chalk

Pebble

To play this game without scoring, try throwing your pebble on to each square in turn, from one to ten and back again. The first to get there and back is the winner. This boy has just picked up his pebble. Is he about to win his first ever game of Hopscotch?

1 Draw the pitch on the playground with a piece of chalk. Start by drawing one large square and then two more squares on top of it.

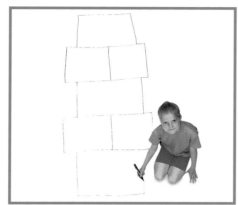

2 Continue drawing the squares in this pattern until you have drawn ten squares. Starting at the first square, number the squares one to ten.

3 The first player throws a pebble, aiming it so that it lands in a high scoring square. If it lands outside the squares, this player will miss a turn.

4 If the pebble lands inside a square, the player hops on to the first square. Try hard to keep your balance and not to step on the lines.

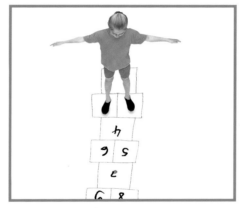

5 The player then jumps with both feet on to the next pair of squares and continues hopping and jumping until the pebble square is reached.

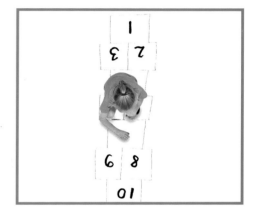

6 From the square before the pebble's square, the player picks up the pebble, jumps over the pebble's square and then continues to the end.

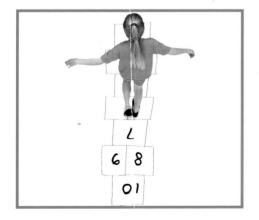

7 At the top, the player turns round and goes back to the start. If there is no mistake, the player scores the points that the pebble landed on.

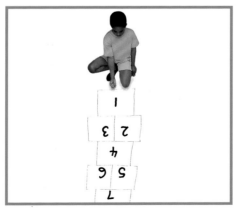

8 The next player aims the pebble for a high scoring square. This player will hop and jump to the pebble in the same way as the first player.

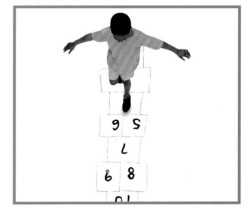

9 If the pebble lands on a double, the player must stand on one leg to pick up the pebble. Whoever scores the most points wins.

Skittles

These skittles are made out of old plastic fizzy drinks bottles or water bottles that have been washed out and recycled. The game is easy to play and can be played outdoors or indoors using a soft ball. To play the game, line the skittles up in a triangle shape and try to knock them all down with one throw. You can play this game with as many people as you like.

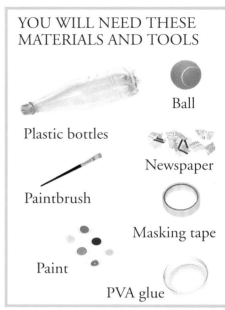

YOU WILL NEED THESE MATERIALS AND TOOLS

Plastic bottles

Ball

Paintbrush

Newspaper

Masking tape

Paint

PVA glue

This boy has scored a strike! He has knocked down all the skittles with one throw of the ball. As a reward he will have another throw.

1 Remove the lid of the bottle. Scrunch a piece of newspaper into a ball shape and attach it to the top of the bottle with strips of masking tape.

2 Mix equal amounts of glue and water and paint it all over the bottle. Cover the bottle with two layers of torn newpaper. Make six skittles.

3 Leave the bottles to dry overnight in a warm place. When the paper has dried, paint the bottles a bright colour and leave the paint to dry.

4 Decorate each skittle with lots of colourful patterns and shapes to make them eye-catching. Leave the paint to dry before playing the game.

5 To play the game, arrange six skittles so that they make a triangle shape. Place one in the first row, two in the second and three at the back.

6 From a line about 5m away, throw the ball at the skittles (you can either stand or kneel). Score the number of skittles you knock down.

7 The next player then picks up the skittles that the first player knocked down and arranges them into the triangle shape.

8 The next player then throws the ball at the skittles and writes down the score. The winner is whoever knocks down the most skittles with one throw.

You can paint your skittles with lots of different patterns, or paint them all in the same pattern to make a set.

Musical Spots

This is fun to play at a birthday party. If the weather is sunny it can be played outdoors. If you do not have any coloured paper to make the spots with, use sheets of newspaper instead. Ask an adult before borrowing a music system. Do not play Musical Spots on a slippery floor because the spots will move about and could cause an accident.

This girl's quick reactions have helped her win this game of Musical Spots. You could have a little victory dance of your own when you win the game.

YOU WILL NEED THESE
MATERIALS AND TOOLS

Coloured paper

Felt tip pen   Scissors

1 Draw a large circle on a piece of coloured paper and cut it out to make a spot. You will need one for each player plus one extra spot.

2 Lay the spots out on the floor so that they are spread out from each other and there is enough room to move in between them.

3 Ask a friend who is not playing the game to be in charge of the music. When the music starts, begin to dance around the spots but not on them.

4 When the music stops, everyone quickly jumps on to a spot. You are not allowed to jump on to the same spot as another player.

5 It is time now to make this game really difficult. Remove two spots, so that you have one less spot than the number of players.

6 When the music begins, start dancing and try to stay near the spots. Otherwise you will not have a spot to stand on when the music stops.

7 The music stops again and the players jump on to a spot. The unlucky player who does not have a spot to jump on to is out of the game.

8 Carry on until there is only one spot left and two players. When the music stops, whoever lands on the spot first is the winner of the game.

The spots do not have to be exact circles, just big enough for someone to stand on.

Moving Targets

This game is great fun to play both indoors and outdoors. Each player throws a ball at the colourful shapes on the other players' T-shirts and caps. The aim of the game is to throw the ball at the highest scoring shape and hope that it sticks. The winner is the player with the highest score. To start the game, decide which player will throw the ball. Everyone else will be the moving targets.

Fawwaz has scored a direct hit on a cap. He gets ten points – the highest score, for this hit.

1 Draw a star, a square and a circle on three different coloured pieces of felt. Cut out one of each shape, the same size, for each of the players.

2 Cut three strips of loop-sided Velcro the same length for each shape. Stick the strips of Velcro on to the centre of the felt shapes.

3 Glue the star to the cap. Put a sheet of paper inside the T-shirt, glue the circle on the front and the square on the back. When dry, remove the paper.

4 Cut two strips of hook-sided Velcro long enough to go around the ball. Stick them on with glue, holding the strips in place while the glue dries.

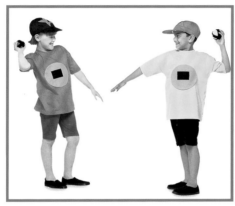

5 When all the glue is dry, everyone puts on an outfit and runs around in an open space, aiming their balls at the other players' T-shirts and caps.

6 If your ball lands on a shape, write down the score (square = 4 points, circle = 6 points and star = 10 points). Continue playing the game.

7 The main target is the cap as it has the most points. Keep playing until everyone is tired, then add up the scores to see who has won.

Use an old T-shirt and an old cap to make your outfit. The felt shapes should be the same size for everyone to make the game fair.

Fruity Boules

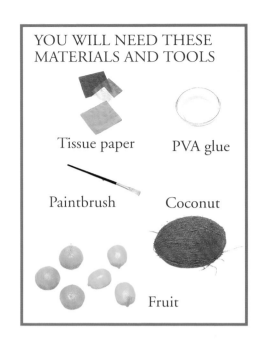

This game is best played outdoors on a flat open space. There is no limit to how many people can play, but each player should have at least two boules or pieces of fruit. The aim of Fruity Boules is to roll the boule or fruit as close as possible to the target boule. If at the end of the game, more than one boule or fruit looks as if it is the same distance from the target, use a ruler to measure the distance accurately. The closest is the winner.

Georgina is the winner of this game of Fruity Boules. Her lemon is touching the target, a large coconut. Before it is your turn, practise rolling your fruit to find out how its shape affects how it rolls.

1 Make a tissue ball. Mix even amounts of glue and water, and cover the ball. Squeeze out the glue and leave to dry. Make two for each player and one target.

2 Glue on small pieces of coloured tissue paper, completely covering each boule. Cover one boule in a different colour to make the target.

3 When the boules are dry, agree on a starting line. Throw the target boule first. A crouching position makes it easy to aim the boule accurately.

4 The first player then rolls one of their boules and tries to get it as near to the target as possible. If you overshoot, roll the boule more gently.

5 The next player then rolls one of their boules at the target. When everyone has had their first go, each player in turn rolls a second boule.

6 When everyone has thrown two boules, the players go over to the target. The player whose boule is the nearest to the target is the winner.

7 The game can also be played with round or oval fruit, like oranges and lemons. The target fruit – a coconut is perfect – is rolled first.

8 Each player is given two identical fruits. Lemons are tricky to roll, so give them to an expert. The first player then rolls their first fruit.

9 The players take it in turn to roll their fruits at the target coconut. The player who rolls their fruit nearest to the target is the winner.

35

Hoop Shoot

This game can be played outdoors or in a school hall. It can be played with a group of friends divided into teams or you can practise goal shooting by yourself. Play Hoop Shoot with a light plastic ball, not a heavy basketball, as the hoop is not very sturdy. Make sure the ball you use fits through your hoop.

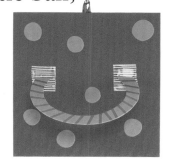

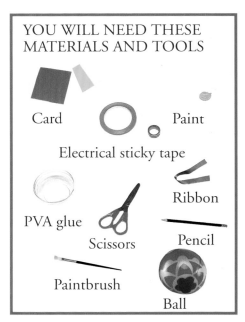

YOU WILL NEED THESE
MATERIALS AND TOOLS

Card   Paint

Electrical sticky tape

Ribbon

PVA glue

Scissors   Pencil

Paintbrush

Ball

The blue team have scored a goal – hooray! Set a time limit of about 30 minutes for your game of Hoop Shoot.

1 Draw a hoop, large enough for your ball to fit through, on two pieces of card and cut them out. Make two hoops if you have two teams.

2 Bend the ends of each hoop out as shown. Glue the hoops, but not the ends, together. Cut a 45cm x 45cm piece of card for the back of the hoop.

3 Paint both sides of the hoop in a plain colour and leave the paint to dry. Decorate the hoop by wrapping electrical sticky tape around it.

4 Cut a length of ribbon 12cm long. Glue the ribbon on to the back of the card to make a loop. Cover the ribbon ends with electrical sticky tape.

5 Glue the hoop on to the card and hold it in place while the glue dries. When the glue has dried, stick electrical sticky tape over each join.

6 Hang a hoop at each end of the pitch and form two teams. Run, bouncing and passing the ball between your team, towards your hoop.

7 When a player gets near the hoop, it is time to shoot a goal. If the ball goes through the hoop, that team scores a point and the game restarts.

8 If the player misses and a member of the other team catches the ball, it is their turn to bounce and pass the ball to their hoop and shoot a goal.

9 The team with the most points wins. If both teams have the same score, have a goal-shooting competition to decide on the winner.

Jumping Elastic

This is a type of skipping game that is played with elastic. It is best played outdoors because you will need lots of space. It is a fun game to play at school breaktime with three of your friends. The fun part of this game is making up your own moves or your own songs to sing along to while you are hopping and jumping.

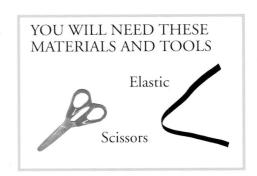

YOU WILL NEED THESE MATERIALS AND TOOLS

Elastic

Scissors

Georgina has thought up a very unusual move for her jumping game! Have a game with your friends to see who can create the craziest moves.

1 Cut a piece of elastic about 4m long and tie the two ends together in a knot. Get two friends to stand inside the loop to stretch it out.

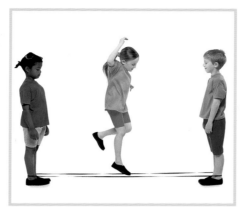

2 Ask your friends to stand with their legs together and the elastic round their ankles. Then, jump in and out of the elastic as fast as you can.

3 Now try crossing the elastic with your feet, then jumping up with the elastic and releasing it. If you are worn out, give someone else a turn.

4 Ask your friends to stand legs astride. Raise the elastic a little and practise jumping in and out.

5 When you are feeling confident, try and do the move described in step 3. Remember to jump high!

6 Raise the elastic to knee height to make the game harder. It will take time to get used to the height of the elastic, so start with easy jumping.

It is lots of fun jumping, hopping and skipping on your own, but even more fun when two friends work out a routine that they can do together.

Croquet

To play this game you will need to make the hoops and a club. The club is not very strong, so it is best to play with a soft ball and not a tennis ball. The game can be played both indoors and outdoors, but remember not to leave the hoops out overnight just in case it rains.

Tom is the first to hit his ball through the final hoop, so he is the winner. Well done Champ!

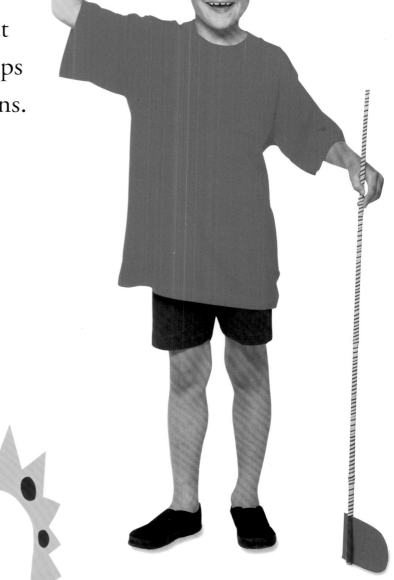

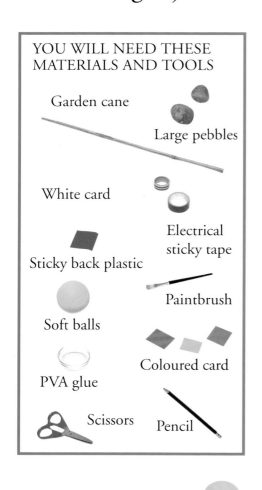

YOU WILL NEED THESE MATERIALS AND TOOLS

Garden cane

Large pebbles

White card

Electrical sticky tape

Sticky back plastic

Paintbrush

Soft balls

Coloured card

PVA glue

Scissors   Pencil

1 To make the club, decorate the garden cane by wrapping electrical sticky tape around it. If the cane is too long, ask an adult to cut it to size.

2 Cut the card to make the head of the club. Cover it with a piece of sticky back plastic larger than the card. Snip edges and fold to back of card.

3 Attach the cane to the card with electrical sticky tape. Cover the back of the card and the bottom of the cane with sticky back plastic.

4 To make a hoop, cut out two pieces of coloured card the same shape. Decorate them with paper spots in a different colour paper.

5 Fold the ends of each hoop out, as shown, and glue the two sides together. Make sure not to glue the ends together. Leave the glue to dry.

6 Make as many hoops as you want. Arrange the hoops in a course on the ground and support each one with a large pebble or something heavy.

7 Toss a coin to see who starts and agree on a starting line. The first player aims their ball at the first hoop. Leave the ball wherever it stops.

8 Then the next player has a go at aiming their ball at the first hoop. When everyone who is playing has had a go, it is the first player's turn again.

9 When you hit your ball through the first hoop, aim for the second hoop and so on. Whoever hits their ball through the last hoop first, wins.

41